Decorative Walls

in a weekend

Decorative Walls

in a weekend

Salli Brand

MEREHURST

For Henry Kus, with whom I am incurably in love, who took a giant leap of faith with me when I decided to give up life in the City in order to pursue a career in decorative art and has encouraged me ceaselessly so far; with thanks for the support, spiritual and physical, and for standing by as I became someone quite different from the woman he first met.

Acknowledgements

Thanks to Dominic Blackmore for superb photography and an even temper, to funky Nel Lintern for single-handedly making these rooms look so great (and letting me take the flowers home), and to Adrian Martindale and Albert Thompson who organized, carried, painted, drove and named me Miss Mustang! To Harry and Audrey Hazelwood for letting us invade their home and, finally, enormous thanks to Sara Colledge for being a tireless and enthusiastic senior editor.

First published 1996 by Merehurst Limited,
Ferry House, 51-57 Lacy Road, London, SW15 1PR

Copyright © 1996 Merehurst Limited

ISBN 1-85391-519-X

A catalogue record for this book is available from the British Library.

Editor: Geraldine Christy
Designer: Anthony Cohen
Photographer: Dominic Blackmore
Stylist: Nel Lintern
Artworks: Brihton Illustration

Colour separation by Dot Gradations, England
Printed in Italy by New Interlitho S.p.A.

Contents

Introduction

Y ou can do it! Decorative walls need not be complicated to paint or require great skill to look wonderfully effective and even more satisfying to the person who creates them. All the projects in this book are feasible for an absolute beginner. Many of them involve only products and tools with which we are all familiar on a day-to-day decorating basis. Some of the projects will introduce you to more unusual materials or specialist brushes, but even these are quite easy to obtain.

I cannot emphasize strongly enough (probably to the annoyance of my fellow professional decorative artists) that there are no rules in decorative art. There are definitely no rights or wrongs. All that is required is for you to be happy with the room you create. Of course, you need to use products that will last, dry in a reasonable amount of time and not wash away, but these aspects are explained in the projects that follow. Indeed, there are times when I invent a new paint technique for my clients and there are many happy accidents. The frottage project on page 8 was suggested to me by my partner (who is not a painter) when he looked over my shoulder at my Saturday afternoon dabblings. We liked it so much that we have put it in this book.

Decorative artists are among the best keepers of secrets I have met. Just as a restaurant owner will not divulge his recipes, so a decorative artist will not tell you many of the tricks of the trade. We prefer to paint marble columns in solitude and we can be seen crouching low over our woodgraining, just in case someone sees how easy it really is. This book is about sharing some of those secrets. Every

beautiful hand-painted piece you see in homes, offices or bars, for example, is just that – painted by hand. Somebody has started with a blank wall or item and has walked away leaving something looking quite different. Why not you?

'I can't draw' is a cry I hear so many times. Well, neither can I. I can probably manage an ivy leaf or a basic cube, but not much else. I manage by referring constantly to books, line drawings and the trusty photocopier that features in three of the projects in the book. A useful trick often practised by theatre set designers is to take a slide photograph of your subject and project it onto the wall. Then draw round it. This is just one example of finding alternative ways to achieve your ends.

This book will introduce you to a wide variety of ideas and techniques that you can apply as shown or develop further. The Anaglypta hallway project on page 12 shows a gilding technique that can be used for gilding larger items such as lamps and furniture with a little practice. The mosaic border on page 40 is a basic introduction to the art of mosaic; if you buy yourself a pair of 'Japanese nippers' for cutting the pieces you could create a masterpiece.

A word about your safety – paint products can be flammable and even toxic (although much less so nowadays). Always read the instructions on the container and work in well-ventilated areas. In a perfect world you really should wear gloves; I always do for the messier techniques. At least wear a barrier cream on your hands. My doctor advised me to try the creams that are sold to protect babies from nappy rash and I can endorse these as the best barrier creams I have found so far.

Finally, remember that you are dealing only with paint, paper and fabric. If you do not like a decorative effect you can paint over it or take it down in no time. When your work is finished, decide for yourself if you like it and if you can live with it. If you do, and if you can, then keep it. One of my friends once said of an unusually and expressively painted dining room in my last home, 'It will be really nice when it's finished.' I had finished it. I think I was the only person who ever ate in that room who loved it, but it stayed. I miss that dining room.

Surrender a weekend and you can have any of the decorative walls featured in this book. Be sure to reward yourself with a favourite indulgence when it is done. Most of all, enjoy your weekend – decorating should be fun.

Sally Brand

Frottage on a Roman vase

Almost hidden under the paint is the image of a Roman vase, achieved with the aid of a photocopier! The process is quick to do and the result looks most effective.

This adventurous-looking wall treatment is suitable for rough or irregular walls and, surprisingly, requires little skill. It is a messy job, though, so be sure to cover your floors well before you start. The secret of this technique is to mix the paints used to colour the design quite thinly to allow the shading from the photocopy to show through. The vase painted here is over 1 m (3 ft) high and was enlarged from a design that is no more than 20 cm (8 in). If you would like to copy this design, you will find templates for the vase on page 72.

Head for the architecture section of the library when seeking out your image. Numerous books are published for artists and architects that contain endless pages of source pictures like the one used here. Alternatively, you can find inspiration in catalogues of garden statuary. Even colour photographs enlarge well on a black and white photocopier.

You will be able to complete one large design and all the walls of an average-sized room easily in a weekend, and still have time for shopping while the layers of paint dry. This effect also looks great on just one wall and you can add more designs under the paint if you wish.

It is fun to experiment with colour, too; try painting the photocopy in verdigris colours and frottaging over it in bold tones of terracotta.

Prepare the walls by painting them in white vinyl silk for this effect. A matt surface is not suitable.

An alternative to varnishing the design before applying the glaze is to apply a diluted solution of PVA glue, which is quick drying.

Day One

Step 1

Enlarge your chosen design in sections using a photocopier until it is the size you require. Assemble the design carefully and piece it together with glue. Trim off any white edges or surplus from the sections of the photocopy as you go.

Step 2

Paint the design using artist's acrylic colours. I used yellow ochre, Naples yellow, buff titanium and burnt sienna for this design. Keep the paints well thinned with water so that the photocopy design shows through. Your painting does not need to be perfect, a base of colour is all you need to apply; remember that you will be hiding it under three layers of frottage.

Step 3

Cut out the design around the outline. Then apply a generous amount of wallpaper paste to the back of the design, being careful not to tear it. Also apply some paste to the wall where the design will be positioned. Let the paste soak in for two or three minutes, then gently position your painted design on the wall and smooth it down with a brush or cloth. Press out any large bubbles but do not worry if the design is a bit wrinkly – it will dry flat. Leave it to dry for the rest of the day. While the design dries, follow steps 5–9 on the other walls in the room.

Step 4

When the wallpaper paste is completely dry (speed it up with a fan heater if you like) varnish the design carefully. If you wish you can skip this step, but the varnish coating means that as you apply the frottage you can wipe away any areas you find too heavy. Without the coat of varnish the glaze will be on for good and you will not be able to adjust it.

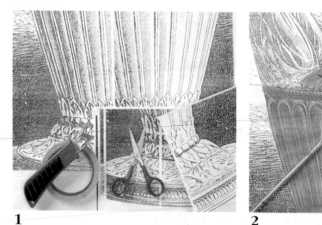

1

2

3

5

6

7

8

Day Two

Step 5

Mix up three separate coloured paint kettles of glaze by adding one part eggshell paint in the colour you have selected to one part transparent oil glaze and about two parts of white spirit. The glaze should be about as thin as milk and no thicker than single cream. Add a teaspoon of dryers to each colour. The colours I have used here are a medium shade of dull yellow, a dusty terracotta and a pale dusty yellow.

Step 6

Using one colour, 'colourwash' the wall in sections about one metre (3 ft) square at a time with a large brush; apply the paint with broad criss-cross strokes, quite wet but not so wet that it runs. Colourwash over your painted design, too.

9

Step 7

Immediately press a piece of torn newspaper onto the wet paint. Pat it down and pull it away from the wall. This gives a random, blotchy effect. Some of the newsprint will come off onto the wall in patches, adding to the effect. This is why you should avoid using newspaper with colour pictures.

Step 8

Continue colourwashing all around the walls, working quickly. Try not to let any

of the edges dry before moving onto the next section as this creates a 'watermark'. The same piece of newspaper goes a long way. You should be able to colourwash all around the room in less than one hour. Let this coat of paint dry for a couple of hours, and when this first layer of frottage is dry or just tacky to the touch, repeat the whole process in a darker colour. I painted the darker glaze quite heavily

around the bottom of the room and around the design for a slightly shaded effect. When applying this second colour avoid any straight lines when blotting with your piece of newspaper.

Step 9

Finally, repeat the process with a lighter colour, adding only the odd patch of paint here and there.

Embossed paper and verdigris hallway

This colourful hallway shows how embossed papers, often used to cover defects, can be livened up quickly and easily to give a new look to your home.

Embossed wallpaper is a useful way of hiding a multitude of irregularities. Inheriting this kind of paper in a new home may be a sign of uneven or cracked plaster and it may take a great deal of time to remedy the problem if you choose to strip off the paper. The effect illustrated here was actually painted onto brand new paper. Halfway through the job, however, I realized how often I have seen embossed papers on the walls of my friends' new homes, looking rather drab and crying out to be given a new lease of life.

The design of the paper is low lighted with a simple glaze technique. This shows up the design more strongly and adds a transparent tint.

I chose three tones of one colour for the base paints – light apricot for above the rail, mid apricot for below the rail and deep terracotta for the background of the border. For the two glazes I used mid apricot – the same colour as the dado rail and the base paint below the rail – for the top glaze, and dark apricot for below the dado rail.

The blue-green verdigris border is painted with a technique that can also be used for small items of furniture. The table shown here was painted in the same way as the border, but in lighter tones of the colours.

Verdigris is actually the name given to the corrosion that occurs on copper that has been exposed to the damp or left out in the elements. The verdigris decoration here has tiny spots of real copper peeking through the paint here and there. It is applied using the same basic gilding technique that you would use on items such as lamp bases.

Planning your time

DAY ONE

AM: Paint the base coats; paint the base of the border

PM: Apply glaze to both sections of the wall

DAY TWO

AM: Apply copper leaf to border

PM: Verdigris the border

Tools and materials

Good quality cotton rags

5 litres vinyl silk paint in a light apricot colour

2.5 litres vinyl silk paint in a mid apricot colour

Paint roller for textured walls or decorator's brush

1 litre vinyl silk paint in deep terracotta

2 small (0.5 litre) cans of oil-based transparent glaze

0.5 litres eggshell paint in each of the two glaze colours

White spirit

Artist's oil paint (only if you stain the glaze for below the dado rail rather than buy a ready-mixed eggshell; see step 1)

Gilder's copper transfer leaf

Small bottle of gilder's 'size' – water or oil based

Large bottles (about 300 ml) artist's acrylic paints in phthalocyanine green, raw umber and white

Small tube artist's acrylic paint in cerulean blue

Good quality paintbrush

1 pot of rottenstone

Masking tape

Day One

Step 1

Paint the base coats of paint above and below the dado rail using vinyl silk paint. It is important that you do not use a matt finish or the glazing will not work. Use a thick roller or a decorator's brush for this. Two coats are recommended and you will find the first coat is dry enough to re-paint once you have completed the whole room. Work from the top down.

Paint the background of the border with deep terracotta vinyl silk or eggshell paint (eggshell is available from paint suppliers in smaller quantities and you have time to leave it to dry overnight).

Mix the glaze for the section above the dado rail (see photo 1); this should be slightly darker than the base paint – mix 0.5 litres of scumble glaze with 0.5 litres of eggshell paint in your chosen colour and 0.5 litres of white spirit. The mixture should be as thin as milk and no thicker than single cream. If it is too thick, add a drop more white spirit. The eggshell paint used here is the same colour as the base coat used for the section below the dado rail.

Mix the glaze for the section below the dado rail. Use a separate ready-made colour of eggshell paint for this if you wish; it should be darker than the base paint used below the dado rail. Alternatively, use the same glaze as before, as I have done here, and add a rounded teaspoonful of artist's oil colour in burnt sienna. This results in a darker glaze.

1

2

3

Step 2

Take a deep breath – glazing needs to be done fast. Working on the section above the dado rail, apply glaze with a decorator's brush to the wall in sections about 1 m (3 ft) square. It is easier to work as a pair, with one person applying the glaze and the other wiping it off (see step 3).

Step 3

Immediately wipe away the glaze with a cotton rag folded into a flat pad. Most of the glaze will come away, revealing the base colour, but the glaze will remain in the recessed pattern of the wallpaper. Apply and wipe off the glaze all over the wall, working fast from one section to the next. It is important not to let the edges of a section start to dry before working on the section next to it or you will create a mark where the glaze overlaps. Stop for tea only when you reach a corner! This glazing should take only about an hour and a half for the top section of the whole room. Similarly apply and wipe off glaze on the section below the dado rail using the darker glaze.

Day Two

Step 4

Applying the copper transfer leaf as described in steps 5 and 6 is one of the basic methods for gilding any item. You need to work on a smooth base as brush stokes will show through metal leaf, and to overlap the leaf as you cover the item you are decorating. Use a very soft brush to remove the excess from the overlaps and touch up any cracks by brushing metal powder into them (the same colour as your transfer leaf). You will need to protect your gilding with spray varnish.

Step 5

With a small brush, apply patches of gilder's size at random onto the border. These patches should be different sizes, from about 2 cm (¾ in) to about 4 cm (1½ in) in diameter.

Step 6

Once the size has become tacky, press a piece of copper transfer leaf face down onto a patch, pat it down with your fingers and then peel away the backing paper. As you remove the paper some of the copper will stick. Brush the copper patch with a soft brush or piece of cotton wool to remove any excess copper. Repeat this on all of your patches of size. One sheet of copper goes a long way and you do not need a fresh sheet for each patch.

4

5

6

Step 7

Mix two tones of verdigris green paint using artist's acrylics – you will need about half a cup of each. Use a good squirt of pthalocyanine green, about half as much raw umber, a tiny drop of cerulean blue and a good squirt of white. It is best to check you have the colour right on a piece of paper before mixing the larger quantities. The lighter shade needs more white.

Step 8

Working in sections about 25 cm (10 in) long, stipple on some of the lighter shade of verdigris colour with a firm dabbing motion. Follow a general diagonal flow, rather than applying the paint in blobs. Leave about half of the base paint exposed.

7

Applying the glaze

To avoid marks where the sections of glaze overlap you must work fast. Work in square sections and try to remember where the 'oldest' edge is; this forms the edge of your next section. Bring the glaze work at the corners of the room to a neat finish and you can stop for a rest. It is easier to work as a pair; with one person applying the glaze and the other wiping the glaze off.

8

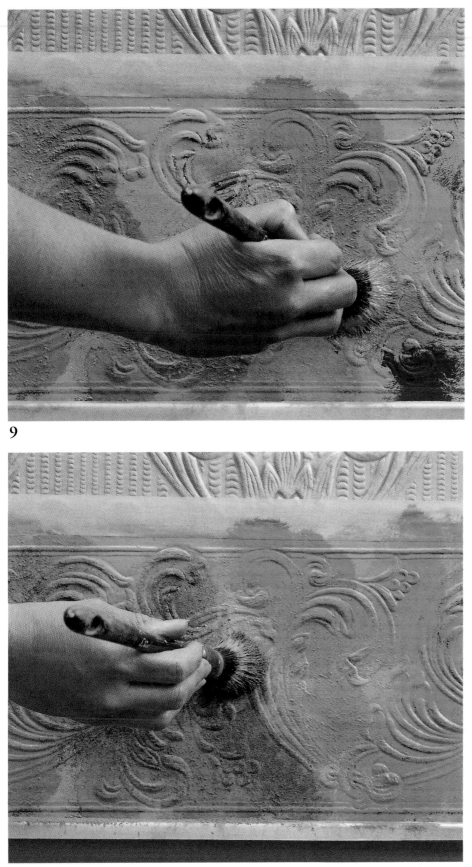

9

10

Step 9

Immediately repeat this, stippling the darker verdigris paint into the remaining strips of base colour. Stipple over your copper leaf but leave tiny 'glints' of it to shine through. You should have covered the whole section with paint now and none of the terracotta colour will be visible.

Step 10

Dip the tip of your brush (you do not need to use a clean one) into the rottenstone and stipple this onto the wet verdigris paint here and there, following the same general diagonal flow. The rottenstone makes the green paint look old and dirty wherever you apply it. Be sure to cover your floors well as much of the powder may end up on the floor. If your dark glaze below the dado rail is not fully dry cover it with plastic sheeting to prevent any falling rottenstone powder from adhering to it. Blend in the rottenstone until obvious streaks do not show. Your brush will become dirty and caked in pigment but can be wiped clean or washed in water.

Contemporary dado and trimmings

Here is a bright and cheerful treatment for a room. It is incredibly simple to do and relies mostly on the adventurous use of colour for its impact.

The decoration of this room is so simple that it allows you plenty of time during your weekend for other obligations. Probably the most taxing part of this project is deciding on which colours to use. The inspiration for this colour scheme comes from the refurbishment of a local historic market. There, the cast-iron trimmings have been painted in bright leafy greens and vivid purples. Other suggestions were to use desert sand and sky blue tones, intense reds and greens or delicate pastel colours.

The overall effect of the decoration on your walls will depend on the colours you select. The colours used here make a bold statement, resulting in a cheerful, almost pop art, feel. Be brave! The trimmings are so quick to paint that you can always change your mind and re-paint them in different colours.

The trimmings used here are produced commercially from medium density fibreboard (MDF). You can buy them by mail order and they all arrive with detailed instructions. You can, of course, cut your own trimmings with a jigsaw (which can be hired without much extra expense).

Planning your time

DAY ONE

AM: Paint the background colours

PM: Prime the bare wood trimmings; paint the trimmings with two coats

DAY TWO

AM: Fix up dado rail; fix trimmings below dado and above skirting

PM: Fix shelf to wall

Tools and materials

Pre-cut trimmings in sufficient length to go all around your room

Dado rail beading – enough for the whole room

Ready-made shelf with trimming

Mitre block

Small saw

Pencil

Spirit level

Tape measure

Acrylic primer paint

Eggshell paint – 0.5 litres for each colour

Paint dryers

PVA glue or decorative moulding glue

1

2

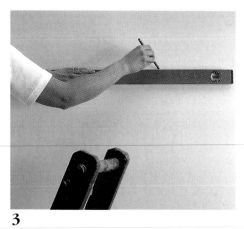

3

Day One

Step 1

Plan your colour scheme on card or
paper before you start if you have any
doubts about how it will work.

Step 2

Paint the background colours with two
coats of emulsion, a different shade
above and below each side of the
position for the dado rail.

Step 3

Using a tape measure and a spirit level,
mark out the positions of each of your
trimmings with a light pencil line.

Step 4

Prime all the pieces of bare wood with
one coat of acrylic primer paint (acrylic
primer dries more quickly than oil-
based primer).

4

Working on plasterboard

If you are attaching the shelf to a
plasterboard wall be sure to use plugs
that have little 'butterflies' along their
length. These plugs open rather like an
umbrella to grip the wall and make a
secure fixing. They are readily available in
DIY stores and may be supplied in the
pack with your shelf.

5

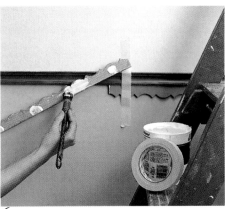

6   **7**

Step 5
Paint all the pieces with eggshell paint. You will need to give them all two coats of eggshell paint, so I suggest you use a tiny drop of dryers in the first coat to speed things up.

Day Two

Step 6
When they are dry, glue the pieces to the wall with PVA or panel glue. Apply the dado rail first. If the corners of the dado you have chosen do not butt up against each other comfortably you may have to cut them to an angle using a mitre block and saw – see the Painted panelled hallway project (page 48) for how to do this. Do not worry if the join is not perfect. This can easily be remedied with a touch of filler and then touched over with paint. When the dado is in position tack two or three small nails through it here and there to hold it in place while the glue dries, or hold it in place with masking tape. Fix your painted trimmings under the dado rail and above the skirting board in the same way. These are very light and you will not need any nails to hold them in place.

Step 7
Fix the ready-made shelf securely to the wall following the instructions in the pack. Make sure that there are sufficient brackets for the shelf to hold the weight of the items you intend to put on it, and that you use wall plugs in any holes you drill.

Finishing off the shelf
....
The shelf shown here was made by the same company that made the trimmings and has a groove cut into the front of it for another row of the carved trim. This just slotted into position by hand. I added a squirt of glue to make sure it stays secure. You can use this trimming pointing upwards to hold items such as plates in place if you choose.

Cheat's border découpage

This delightful découpage idea uses commercial, ready-printed borders. It can be carried out at short notice or makes a suitable project for a rainy weekend.

If you start cutting out the design in the days before your weekend you may well find this project does not even take two days, and if your paintwork is in good condition you do not even have to lift a brush. This is a way of using wallpaper borders to great effect. The overall effect has a gentle flow and if you use a floral or natural subject the border literally seems to grow around your room.

Natural subjects are ideal for this technique as there is no planning and serious measuring to do. This does not mean that the selection of geometrically patterned borders on the market will not work well, but if you choose to use one of these you will need to spend some time working out your arrangement. The edges of a geometric design are likely to be less soft to look at than the one I have used here, but you will still be able to make the design escape from its printed confines so that it enhances the architectural features of your room.

Planning your time

DAY ONE

AM: Paint the base coat

PM: Apply plain strip of commercial border; start cutting out the design

DAY TWO

AM: Finish cutting the design

PM: Glue découpage in place

Tools and materials

5 litres emulsion paint in your base colour

Rolls of commercially printed border, about three and a half times the length of the area you wish to cover

2 large tubes of wallpaper border adhesive or a 500 ml pot of PVA glue

Sharp scissors

Craft knife

Cutting mat or wooden board

Spirit level

Pencil

1

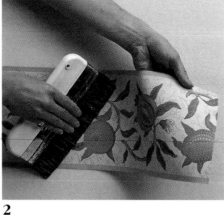

2

3

Day One

Step 1

Select a border for your room that has plenty of potential to spread a design beyond the confines of the way in which it is printed. Floral and natural borders are best for a 'growing' feel, but geometrics and children's borders can also work well. Stripes are not easy to use. Also beware of children's borders that feature trains – trains have to go in straight lines! Select a background colour for your room that is similar to the background on your chosen border. Then paint the walls of the room with at least two coats of emulsion paint and leave to dry.

Step 2

Apply a strip of your chosen border at dado height, making sure that the border is straight by marking a very faint line with a pencil, using a spirit level as a guide.

4

Step 3

Cut out much of the main design from the border. This is time-consuming and close work, but it is worth having a number of cutouts to hand so that you can really make a feature of your découpage strip. You can, of course, cut more as required.

Step 4

Mark a faint line around the room as a guide for the centre of your découpage strip. A dotted line is all you really need, but use a spirit level to keep your guideline straight.

Cutting out

Cutting out large quantities of border may make your hands ache! To combat the aches and pains try alternating between scissors and a craft knife.

5

Day Two

Step 5

Now start creating your design! All you need to do is brush a little of the border adhesive or PVA glue all over the back of each piece and press it onto the wall (I use a lint-free cloth to do this as I find it cleaner). I test each piece first by holding it up to the wall in order to check that I am happy with the position. You can work at random as shown here, or alternatively, once you are happy with a section about 1 m (3 ft) long, you can repeat its design.

Step 6

Make a feature in corners or around window frames and light fittings by extending the design into clusters. Stand back from your work often and look for hard edges or any areas that do not seem to flow well. Adjust these as necessary by adding more pieces or removing some and moving them around.

Step 7

Cut out several of the smaller pieces of the border design, such as leaves and twigs.

Step 8

As a final touch, glue some of these small pieces around your design as shown here. These little 'escapees' give the whole border a natural effect and are useful for finishing the end of a strip without an abrupt or heavy line. They are also very useful if you need to soften your corner clusters.

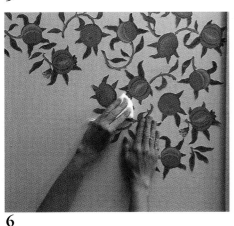

6

7

8

Realistic old stone wall

For anyone who does not live in a castle, but prefers the warmth of modern materials, here is a simple method for creating the look of old stone walls.

S tone walling has a rather mysterious quality to it and this interesting finish lends itself particularly well to smaller rooms that are sometimes difficult to give that extra 'something' to when decorating. In a smaller room, such as a bathroom or cloakroom, the overall effect is rather cabinlike and quite cosy.

The walls do not need to be regularly shaped; indeed, stone walling looks great against sloping ceilings. This decoration is also a useful way of making the most of lumpy walls or walls with a bad plaster finish – often, in fact, the more bumps the better the final look.

The room used here is quite large, with no particular architectural features. I worked with a fairly dark glaze, which has given a very Gothic end result.

A word of warning: once you have done your own room with stone walling be prepared to do it again for your friends!

Planning your time

DAY ONE

AM: Paint the base coat

PM: Mark out the stone; colour each stone with glaze

DAY TWO

AM: Add darker patches to stones; begin shading the edges

PM: Complete shading the edges of the stones; add cracks, crevices and smudges

Tools and materials

Pencil

Ruler

Spirit level

Vinyl silk emulsion paint for the base in a very pale shade of grey (you will need about 5 litres for an average-sized room)

2 litres acrylic scumble glaze

Colourizers for the scumble glaze: 3 white, 1 black and 1 raw umber (if you cannot obtain these, then artist's acrylic paint in tubes will do)

Cellulose sponge

Artist's oil crayons in black, white (about 4 each of these) and a couple of shades of grey and brown. You may prefer to work with wax oil crayons, which are harder and can be sharpened to a fine point.

White spirit

Good quality paintbrush with a flat edge

Small artist's brush

Day One

Step 1

Paint the walls with at least one good coat of light grey emulsion paint. By the time you have completed the room the paint should be dry enough for you to apply a second coat. This second coat is essential if you are painting over a dark colour or pattern. If you are painting over a light colour then one coat will be sufficient so long as the coverage is good. Use a roller or paint pad for speed. Mark out the whole room very lightly in pencil in even brick shapes, using a ruler and spirit level to keep your lines straight. Make the stones the size you wish – those here measure about 65 x 30 cm (26 x 12 in). Remember that the join between the stones alternates on each row. Refer to the main picture for guidance on this if you need to.

Step 2

Mix up about 0.5 litres of grey glaze by adding small quantities of black and white colourizer or artist's acrylic to the scumble glaze in a paint kettle. Stir the mixture well and be careful to add only small amounts at a time as these colours are very powerful. You will only need about three drops or so of black and a couple of good squirts of white.

Step 3

Carefully colour a stone with a paintbrush, taking great care to paint right up to the edges, then immediately dab the stone all over with a torn-off chunk of cellulose sponge. This dabbing removes all of the brush strokes and begins to create the effect of rough stone. Colour all the stones in this way, working at random around the room. When you run out of glaze, mix another 0.5 litres in the same colour; do not worry if it is not exactly the same shade as you are creating a natural look and real stones are not all the same colour.

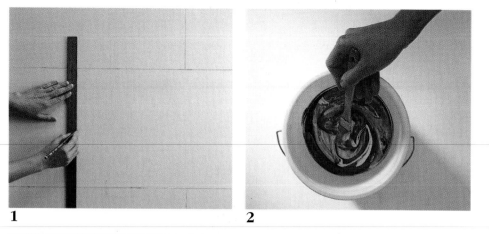

1 **2**

3

4

5

Day Two

Step 4

Now darken your glaze slightly, adding a touch of raw umber for a more dirty effect, and a spot more black. Dab touches of this glaze onto most of the stones, using the sponge. Do not make every stone look the same, but try to create the natural ageing process. I like to make the edges of a number of the stones look dirty and to make patches here and there, sometimes dabbing over half a stone. Avoid painting straight lines as they look unnatural.

Step 5

Make a selection of artist's oil crayons in darker shades than you have used for the painting and some white. These oil-based crayons come in a variety of hardnesses. Softer ones are useful for smudging and broad lines, while harder ones can be sharpened to a fine point for thin lines and cracks.

Highlights and shadows

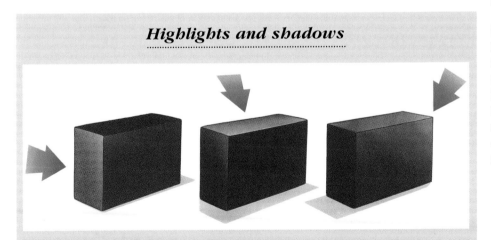

To decide where shadows and highlights fall on an object imagine snow falling from a set direction. The snow settles only on the areas it reaches naturally; it cannot go round corners. Where the snow settles corresponds with highlights and where it cannot reach corresponds with shadows.
Still confused? You can experiment yourself by wetting a three-dimensional item and throwing sugar or talcum powder at it from the direction you choose for the sunlight to be coming from. Where the sugar sticks to the item is highlight; where it does not stick is an area of shadow.

Step 6

Using the white crayon, draw highlights on the areas of the stones where the sunlight would fall naturally. You can decide on this angle for yourself but remember to be consistent for the whole room. Here, the sunlight is coming from above, slightly to the right of the picture. The white crayon goes along the top of each stone and down the crack on the right-hand side of each. Smudge the crayon lines with your finger for a softer effect and round off the corners slightly.

Step 7

Now add the shadows to each stone with a black crayon. This time the shadows are added where the sunlight cannot reach, so I put them on the underneath of each stone, and down the left-hand edge. Soften these with your finger as you make them, to avoid hard lines. Avoid using a ruler for steps 5 and 6 if you can, or the lines will look too defined.

6

Bevelled edges

If you want the edge of each stone to look bevelled then highlight and lowlight with fairly wide crayon lines. For non-bevelled stones your line should be only about 2 mm (¹⁄₁₆ in) wide in each colour. After you have shaded a few stones, stand back from your work and decide if your lines are too thick or thin. You can remove them with white spirit if you are not happy, or smudge them with your fingers to soften them some more.

7

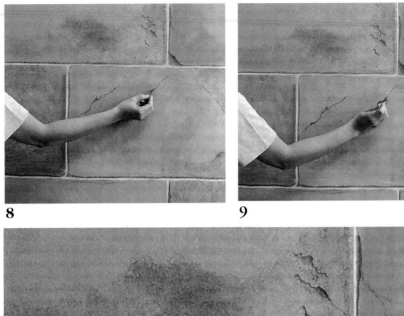

8

9

10

Step 8

Using a black or dark grey crayon add cracks and crevices carefully to a number of the stones; follow the edges of your darker glaze patches for some of them. Make fairly faint wiggly lines for the cracks and add some chips here and there by colouring in small chunks along these lines. These, too, can be highlighted with the white crayon in areas where the sun would catch.

Step 9

Using a fine brush dipped into a drop of white spirit, gently dab at the chips you have drawn to soften them and to blend away any obvious drawing lines.

Step 10

Now and then stand back from your wall while you are working to be sure that your crayon work looks natural. If you draw in any cracks that you do not like rub them out with your fingers and a tiny drop of white spirit. This creates darker smudges that are very effective and leaves the faintest hint of a crack behind the smudge. If you are happy with all of your cracks add some smudges here and there anyway.

Finishing off the stones

When I 'stone wall' in my own home I keep the crayons handy in the room for a few days after the work is complete; then I can add more cracks if I see a stone that looks bare.

Accent colours

Here a deep and rich textured paint effect has been applied to a dado rail, skirting board and ornate cornice, bringing some vibrant colour accents to the room.

Clean lined and uncluttered, this room could almost be an art gallery. It is not always necessary to paper or paint the walls of a room in order to give it a lift. The colour in this room creates interest without being too radical. An accent colour in a room is just that – accent. It is the one striking colour that is specific to the décor. Most homes already have accent colours in two rooms: the bathroom and the kitchen. The colours of the towels in the bathroom and the accessories in the kitchen are perhaps more vivid or deeper than the rest of the décor and yet purchased to belong specifically in that room.

This project takes accent colours a stage further and brings them into the living room as permanent additions. We chose to work in deep red against neutral backgrounds. Another suggestion is to use ultramarine blue on white, which gives a Mediterranean or 'Roman' feeling; or you may wish to try a combination of bottle green on pale yellow, which has a wonderful freshness.

Planning your time

DAY ONE

AM: Test colours on paper; paint base colours on walls

PM: Paint base colours on fixtures

DAY TWO

AM: Glaze cornice with accent colour; glaze skirting and dado rail

PM: Paint extra items in accent colour

Tools and materials

0.5 litres transparent oil glaze

Tubes of artist's oil paint in your chosen colours (the colour here is Indian red with a dash of Paynes grey added to it)

1 litre of vinyl silk paint for the bases in a much brighter colour than you intend the finish to be (I used flame red)

Masking tape

2 small household paintbrushes

Plastic carrier bag

Cotton rag or kitchen cloth

Paint dryers (very important)

Day One

Step 1

Spend some time deciding on your colour scheme. Plan it out on a piece of paper in order to be sure that you will be happy with it. Use tester pots for the base colours. When selecting the accent colour, use traditional paint colours to guide you, either by looking at the tubes of paint in your local art shop or at sets of coloured pencils that are usually produced in traditional colours.

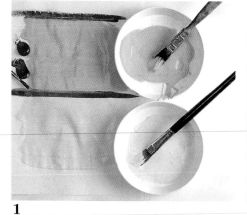

1

2

Step 2

Paint the walls of your room with two coats of emulsion paint.

Step 3

When the walls are completely dry apply masking tape along the edges of the fixtures such as the dado rail, skirting and cornice. Then paint the fixtures with two coats of vinyl silk emulsion in a brighter colour than you intend the finished colour to be.

3

4

Day Two

Step 4

Mix a very thick glaze in a pot, in the colour you choose: put about four large spoonfuls of stirred transparent oil glaze into the pot and add about a spoonful of artist's oil colour. Mix it well – the consistency will be thick and gooey like jam and have a slippery feel to it. Add half a teaspoon of paint dryers. The addition of dryers is very important; artist's oil colours take days, or even weeks to dry without them.

Step 5

Apply the glaze evenly to the cornice and dab out any obvious brush marks by jabbing the tip of your brush over the wet glaze. You do not need to concentrate too much energy on this, just apply a fairly even layer of glaze. Work on a section about 1 m (3 ft) long, then immediately go on to step 6.

5

6

7

8

Step 6

This is like magic! Dab a crumpled up carrier bag over the thick wet glaze and create a textured 'leathery' effect. The bright base colour will peep through the dark glaze where the bag lifts away the glaze. Then repeat steps 5 and 6, working in sections.

Step 7

If you have an ornate cornice, take a clean rag and wipe away the glaze from some of the proud areas of the carving, revealing the base coat of bright paint. This is a traditional technique, known as 'wipe on, wipe off', and is often used in grand buildings. If your cornice is plain, leave it after step 6.

Step 8

For the dado rail, apply an even layer of glaze all along the rail on one wall. Then, starting at one end, press the flat side of your brush firmly into the glaze and run it right along the rail as shown here, from end to end. The brush will leave gentle stripes behind it, giving a delicate dragged effect. Repeat steps 5 and 6 on the skirting board, taking good care to protect the carpet as the oil pigments are very powerful.

Step 9

The room is finished, but the final touch with accent colours is to give the same finish to some of the accessories. Picture and mirror frames and the wastepaper bin are suitable items to paint, as are vases and storage boxes.

9

Paint names

Artist's paints colours are usually given traditional names. This list is not exhaustive but may help you to find the colour you are looking for.

Dark green: Hooker's green or Sap green
Royal blue: Ultramarine blue
Mustard yellow: Yellow ochre
Red: Alizarin crimson or deep red
Ox-blood red: Indian red

Orange: Cadmium red
Sunflower yellow: Cadmium yellow
Dark turquoise green: Phthalocyanine green
Tan: Burnt sienna
Dark brown: Raw umber
Cream: Titanium buff, unbleached titanium
Bright blue: Cerulean blue
Dark blue: Prussian blue

Lining with fabric panels

Sumptuous toile de jouy fabric lines the walls of this room, creating the style and atmosphere of a stately home or the setting for a period novel.

I t is easier than you think to line the walls of your room with fabric panels. The frames used in this project were made by a joiner. You could make your own but the extra cost for such simple joinery is minimal. If you do decide to make your own panels they should be perfectly square at the corners and strengthened with one or two cross batons as shown in the photograph for step 1.

Find the centre of the walls and use this as the centre point for the panels. Then decide how many panels you would like on each wall and how wide each one needs to be to fit. For example, the wall here was just over 4.5 m (15 ft) long and just over 2.4 m (8 ft) high. I chose to have six panels, each 0.75 m (2½ ft) wide and 2.4 m (8 ft) high so that they would fit between the floor and ceiling. Keep to the same width of panel for the whole room if you can. Centralize the panels on each wall and slot thinner ones in at the corners.

When you buy your fabric you need to allow enough to match up seams. This is easy; the sales assistants in the stores are trained to do these calculations! Tell the assistant how many panels you are making and the height of each. The fabric I chose was 137 cm (54 in) wide and so I had plenty of extra at the sides of each panel. I lost only about 1 m (3 ft) in length matching up the design.

If you are lining walls with plain fabric or fabric with a small pattern in the weave then no complicated calculations are required. Just buy 1 m (3 ft) extra to allow for wrapping around the wood.

Planning your time

DAY ONE

AM: Plan the position of all your panels; staple hook and loop fastener to the wall

PM: Begin covering panels

DAY TWO

AM: Continue covering panels

PM: Staple hook and loop to the panels; press the panels into position

Tools and materials

Wooden frames (those shown here were made by a joiner) conforming to the measurements of your room. Remember to keep the panels narrower than the width of your chosen fabric.

Staple gun and plenty of staples

Drawing pins

Sufficient hook and loop fastener to go around the outside of all of your panels

Sufficient fabric to cover the panels (allow for matching of seams and drops)

Sharp scissors

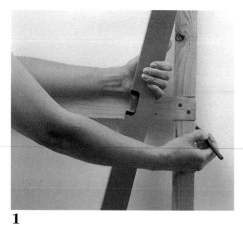

1

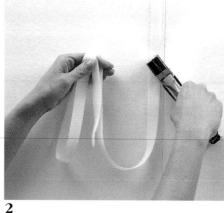

2

3

Day One

Step 1

Position all your panels around the room and make sure that they fit. Then mark the position of each, using a spirit level or plumb line to keep the drops straight.

Step 2

Using a staple gun, staple a strip of the roughest side of the hook and loop fastener to the walls, with the hooks facing you, just inside the lines you have marked to show the edges of the panels.

Step 3

Lay out your fabric and plan how the seams will match. Do not cut the fabric into sections until you are sure you are not wasting more than is necessary. Cut the fabric for the height of the first panel, plus a bit extra to wrap around the wood and then cut the fabric for the other panels as you progress.

Step 4

Now spend some time positioning your fabric onto the panels (I used some drawing pins first). Stretch the fabric around the panels, keeping it straight and checking the front often. Staple it onto the back of the panels. As soon as you have made one panel you will be able to work much faster and with much more confidence.

4

Fitting panels into a corner

Leave a gap at the corners that is exactly the same measurement as the depth of the wood used to make the panels; mine were made from 5 x 2.5 cm (2 x 1 in) timber so I left a 2.5 cm (1 in) gap. This will allow the panels to fit snugly against each other and the pattern to line up.

Day Two

Step 5

Make the corners as neat as you can, folded like wrapping paper on a parcel. The corners should not be bulky. Line your panels up around the room and check that you are happy with them. Adjust any that are not quite right.

Step 6

Cut away the spare fabric from the back of each panel.

Step 7

Now staple a strip of the softer side of the hook and loop fastener all around the edges of each panel, allowing 12 mm (½ in) or so at each edge (to correspond with where you stapled the hook and loop fastener to the wall). Keep the fuzzy side facing towards you. Your staples should be about 15 cm (6 in) apart.

Step 8

The moment of truth! Press each panel into position firmly on the wall. Work your way all around the edge with your hands, pressing hard as you go. Sit back, admire (and eat cake).

5

6

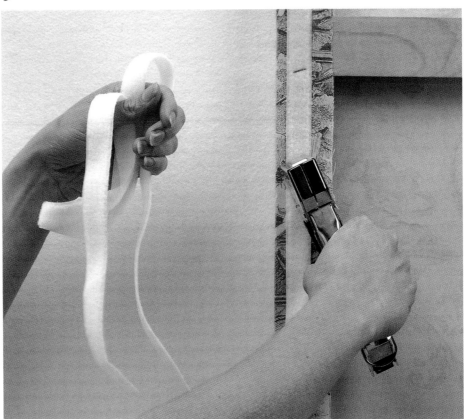

7

Buying fabric

When choosing your fabric remember that it must be lightweight (heavy fabric will pull the panels away from the wall). Fabric with little or no stretch to it is easier to keep straight as you stretch it onto the panels.

Preventing fraying

If you think you will be removing the fabric from the panels regularly for washing it may be worth overlocking the edges on a sewing machine to prevent fraying.

8

Mosaic bathroom border

The art of mosaic dates back thousands of years. This sparkling mosaic border is made using traditional methods and has livened up an otherwise plain bathroom.

Surrender your weekend to this enjoyable project and you may well find you become a mosaic enthusiast. You may even decide to develop further into the art of mosaic and start cutting your pieces. As a start, though, this design involves no cutting.

In the days leading up to your weekend visit a mosaic supplier, or phone one for a brochure. Select your tesserae (for that is what the little squares are called) from an awe-inspiring range of colours and materials. When you get home, put the sheets of tesserae in a bowl of water for ten minutes and the backing paper will peel away, leaving you with handfuls of beautiful shiny squares that you will not be able to resist playing with. The tesserae used for this design are made of vitreous glass and come from Italy; they are water and heat resistant. You can walk on them too.

The mosaics here are 'grouted' with concrete, which is the traditional setting material for mosaics and brings out their colours well, but you may use ordinary tile grout if you prefer.

Planning your time

DAY ONE

AM: Paint the background of your wall

PM: Work out your design and start sticking it into position

DAY TWO

AM: Finish sticking your design in place

PM: Grout the design with concrete

Tools and materials

Sufficient tesserae to complete your design. This design took five sheets of green, one sheet each of white and bright blue, and two sheets of dark blue with copper tinges.

Glue
(Any fairly quick drying type will do. Try EVA glue, a glue gun or border adhesive.)

Emulsion paint for your background – 2.5 litres is sufficient if you are working above tiles

Paintbrush

Small bag of ready-mixed concrete, which is a mixture of sand and cement powder

Gloves (very important)

Strips of polythene to cover your work with

Soft cloths

Large, old bowl for mixing concrete

Water

Old paintbrush

1

Day One

Step 1

Paint the background of your wall with two coats of emulsion paint. Keep some for later use.

Step 2

Spend some time planning your design on a piece of paper. When you are happy with it, keep the design on one side as a reference.

Step 3

Begin gluing the tesserae in place using your chosen glue. If you are using EVA glue then put a dab on the back of each piece before sticking it to the wall. With a glue gun or border adhesive, put the dabs of glue on the wall. Leave a small gap between each piece.

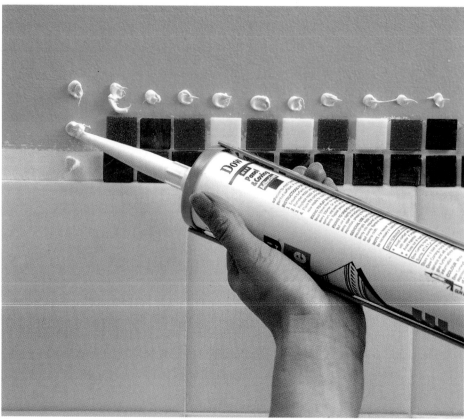

2

3

Becoming an expert

Want to develop further? When you buy your tesserae you may also want to acquire a pair of 'Japanese nippers', which are the tool used to cut the pieces into any shape you require. Ask for a quick demonstration of how to use them. Basically, you grip the very edge of your tile with the edge of the nippers and squeeze them together, squeezing the little tile in your free hand at the same time. Practice makes perfect.

4

Day Two

Step 4

When the design is complete, leave it to dry fully for at least an hour. Then mix your concrete: put a few handfuls of the powder into an old bowl and add a very small amount of water. Mix this around with your hands and add more water (if needed) until you have a fairly dry, crumbly mixture. If you get to the stage where you have a soft doughy mix, it is too wet so add some more powder. Concrete can ruin your hands, so wear gloves for these steps.

Step 5

This is messy, so cover your floors well. Take handfuls of the concrete mix and press them into the gaps between the tesserae. Work the mix well into the gaps using swirly motions with your hands.

5

Fitting the tesserae

If your pieces do not fit perfectly up to the corners of the room, adjust the spaces between the tesserae by a tiny (virtually invisible) degree for the last few centimetres.

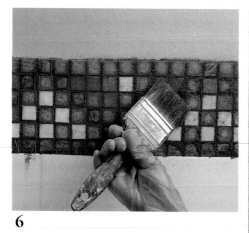

6

Step 6

Brush away the excess lumps of
concrete with your hands and an old
paintbrush.

Step 7

Now moisten a soft cloth in water and
wring it out extremely well. Gently
wipe over the surface of your mosaic to
remove the excess concrete and begin
to clean the design. Wash out the cloth
often and wring it out well every time;
it is important not to wet the concrete
too much. Smooth along the top of
your design as well as you can.

Step 8

Touch up the paintwork, which you
will have smudged with concrete.

7

Cheating

You can, of course, grout mosaic with
ordinary tile grout. It does not bring out
the colours of the tesserae so well and is
actually a bit more fiddly, but cleaner. No
qualification as a mosaic snob if you
cheat though!

8

9

Step 9

Admire your work for a few minutes because, sadly, you have to cover it up for at least two whole days. Concrete needs to be kept moist for this length of time to 'cure'. If you do not do this it will crumble every time you touch it. Cover the design well with polythene or keep it damp by laying damp cloths over it. Spray the design a couple of times with water during the two days, just to be sure it is not drying. Finally, after two days, remove the polythene and allow your design to dry fully.

Step 10

You can clean off any dusty marks on the tiles with patio and path cleaner or hydrochloric acid. Wet the surface and apply the cleaner, which will fizz. Scrub the surface with a stiff brush and rinse well. The shiny surface of the finished mosaic border is practical and attractive.

10

Alternative materials

No local mosaic supplier? Many mosaics, particularly those in public places, are made with pieces of broken china, old pots and small pieces of junk (the workings from old clocks are good). This is not cheating, just another method, and also looks charming.

Painted panelled hallway

An elegant and welcoming hallway in which three different paint effects and carefully painted panels work in harmony with each other to give a clean, smart appearance.

Although they look as if they have been in place for a century or so, even the panels here are new. They are easy to assemble; if you have used a saw before, even for firewood, then you will be able to panel your room with the tricks shown here. You may even decide to go further and panel your doors, too. Before you start, decide how many panels you would like and how much beading you will need. Buy this in lengths from your local DIY store.

The choice of colours for a project such as this is, of course, immense. In this hallway the colours are all shades of the same colour, selected from the paint mixing strips of colours displayed in DIY stores. By choosing from the same strip you can be certain that your colours will go well with each other.

Many homes with panelled walls leave the beading of the panels plain white; in fact so many do so that white beading is almost traditional. You will be stunned by the extra depth that deep colour used on the beading can bring to a room.

This project introduces you to three paint effects – ragging, dragging and bagging – all of which are very simple. Specialist dragging brushes are available from some DIY stores; otherwise from specialist paint suppliers.

Planning your time

DAY ONE
AM: Cut panels
PM: Paint bases; apply panels

DAY TWO
AM: Paint finishes above the dado rail
PM: Bagging below dado rail; paint beading

Tools and materials

Sufficient lengths of beading to make panels, plus one length extra to allow for cutting loss

Border and panel adhesive

Tenon saw

Mitre block

1 litre of transparent oil glaze

0.5 litres of eggshell paint in each of your three chosen colours

2.5 litres of vinyl silk emulsion paint in each of your two chosen base colours

3 large plastic plant saucers

Cotton rags

Three or four plastic carrier bags

Stippling brush (optional)

Dragging brush

Household decorating brush

White spirit

Masking tape

Day One

Step 1

Prime the wood with primer paint if it is bare when you buy it. Cut the beading into accurate lengths using the tenon saw and mitre block as shown here. Take care that your pieces will all be the correct way round and reverse the angle of the cut for the second of two corner cuts.

The photograph shows clearly the correct angle for corner cuts. You will soon get the hang of how the angles should be cut and you have all morning to cut these panels, which allows plenty of time for a couple of mistakes.

Step 2

Paint above and below the dado rail with two coats of vinyl silk emulsion (matt is not suitable for paint finishes) in the colours you have chosen for your base coats. The colours here are a very pale blue-green for the top section and a deeper blue-green for the bottom section (both colours were chosen from the same paint mixing colour strip in a DIY store). Remember that you will be adding an even darker glaze over the paint bases.

Step 3

Now stick your panels into position on the wall using blobs of glue on the backs of the pieces or putting blobs onto the wall. Mark the inside line of each panel with a pencil for guidance. Keep a close eye on the panels you have glued, as they sometimes slip. Secure them with masking tape if they do start to move. Fill any gaps where the corners join with filler or more panel adhesive.

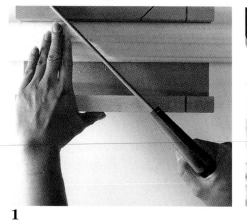

1

2

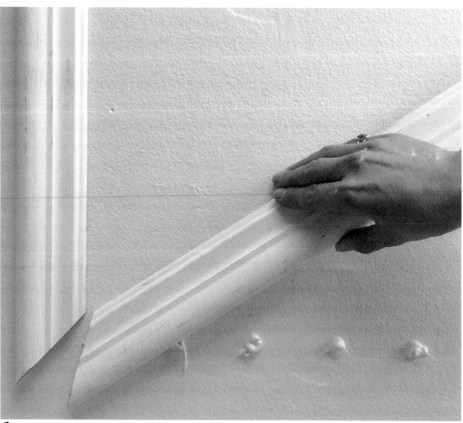

3

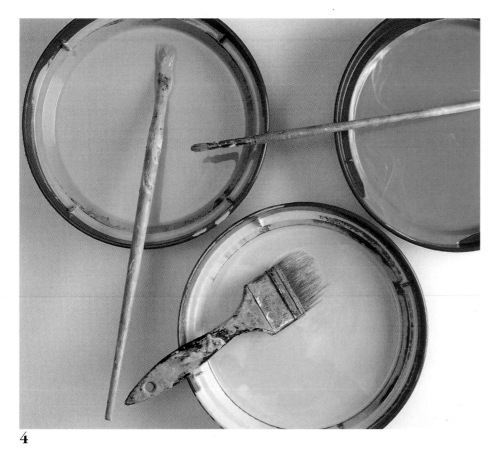

4

5

Day Two

Step 4

Now mix three trays of glaze in your chosen colours; I find plastic plant saucers useful containers. Your colours should be about two or three shades apart on a paint mixing card, and darker than your base paint. Use 1 part transparent oil glaze, 1 part paint and 1 part white spirit. Keep the lightest and darkest glazes quite thick, but thin the medium glaze with a drop more white spirit so that it has the consistency of milk.

Step 5

Brush your lightest glaze all over the inside of one panel and then immediately stipple away the brush strokes with light jabbing motions using a stippling (or household) brush. This stippling is optional but it prevents any of your brush strokes from showing up on the finished work, so gives a more pleasing result.

Glazing

You must work fast with glazing techniques; if not, the glaze will start to dry and you will see a mark where you apply the next section. Working in a pair, with one person applying the glaze and the other person ragging, dragging or bagging overcomes this problem.

Step 6

Immediately dab all over the glaze with a piece of rag, crumpled into a ball. Dab over the whole area of paint quickly and evenly. This paint effect is known as ragging.

Step 7

Apply the thinner, medium colour glaze in manageable strips around the outsides of the panels. Lay the dragging brush onto the wet glaze, starting at the top or side of each section and pull it down through the glaze, pressing firmly as you go. The brush will leave its marks in the glaze and create a delicate striped effect. Use it vertically between the panels and run a horizontal strip of dragging along the top and bottom.

6

Using picture rail

If you use picture rail wood for your panels remember that the chunky, fat section should form the outside edge of each panel.

Dragging

If your dragging starts off well at the beginning of a stroke and then the stripes fade out towards the end of the stroke, first try putting more glaze onto the wall before dragging it. If the stripes still do not look smooth your glaze may be too thick, so add some more white spirit.

7

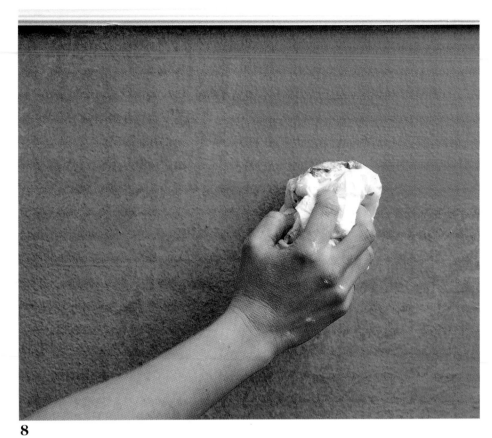

8

Step 8

Using the darkest glaze, which can be quite thick, apply the glaze in sections on the lower part of the room. Turn a plastic carrier bag inside out to prevent any printing ink coming off in your work and crumple it up in your hand. Dab this firmly all over the glaze. The effect is quite 'leathery' in appearance. The further apart the colours are the more the bagging will show up; the ones used here are fairly close to each other, which makes the effect more subtle.

Step 9

Finally, paint your dado rail and beading in a complementary colour.

9

Photocopied designs for a study

Photocopied designs can be used to achieve a huge variety of effects. In this study classical designs are used in warm and spicy colours to create a relaxed atmosphere.

The concept behind this decoration is simple – enlarged photocopies of designs are cut out and stuck to the wall before being painted and varnished. This is a project that can take less than a weekend, or longer, depending on how many images you choose to use and how detailed you make your painting. The only limitation on a project such as this is your imagination.

Once again these images come from architects' source books from the library, but any line drawing will do, even strip cartoons if you are sure that all of the residents in the house share the same sense of humour. Photocopied designs are super for use in children's rooms and geometric patterns work well too. If you would like to copy the designs used here, you will find templates for these line drawings on page 73.

Planning your time

DAY ONE

AM: Select pictures and enlarge on photocopier; cut out designs

PM: Arrange designs on wall; stick them down; begin painting designs

DAY TWO

AM: Paint designs

PM: Highlight designs in gold; varnish

Tools and materials

Good line drawings of your chosen designs

Small sharp scissors or craft knife

Access to a photocopier with enlarging facility

PVA glue or wallpaper paste

Small tubes of artist's acrylic paint in your chosen colours (I used titanium buff, Naples yellow, burnt sienna, burnt umber and gold)

Small soft artist's brushes, about size 4 and size 2 (art shops may try to sell you pure sable brushes at great expense, but imitation sable or nylon are fine for this job)

Small brush for varnishing

Small can of clear varnish (oil-based or polyurethane)

Day One

Step 1

Select good quality line drawings and enlarge them on a photocopier to the size you require. If you are in any doubt about the size, make a selection of copies. Make as many copies as you need and a few spare to allow for any mistakes.

Step 2

Carefully cut out the designs using a small pair of scissors or a craft knife. By clipping about three pages together you can cut more than one image at a time, but be sure they are lined up exactly underneath each other. I prefer to cut one at a time for accuracy.

Step 3

Spend some time arranging your images on the wall securing them lightly with small pieces of masking tape until you are happy with the overall effect and spread. Mark the positions lightly in pencil. Then stick the designs in position using either PVA glue or wallpaper paste. The design should be pressed flat into place and left to dry. Small bubbles and creases in the paper will eventually dry flat.

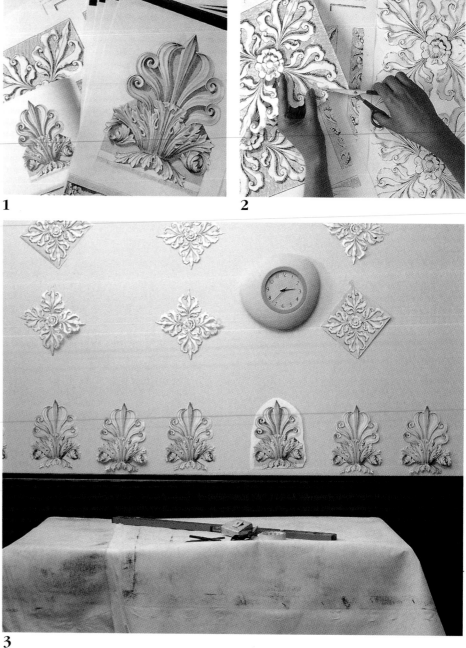

1

2

3

Painting

If you are less brave about painting your designs when they are on the wall you can paint them before sticking them in place. This saves you from having to worry about painting over the edges.

4

Step 4

Paint each design carefully with artist's acrylic paints. Make your paint thin enough (by adding water) for the line drawing to show through. I gave the whole design a wash with buff titanium mixed with a little Naples yellow, then coloured sections with burnt sienna. Finally, I shaded parts with a mixture of burnt sienna and raw umber.

Day Two

Step 5

Highlight the designs with gold artist's acrylic paint, used quite thickly so that it will show. These designs have been painted with quite a large amount of gold so that it can be seen in the photographs - use less than this as it will show up well from different angles in the room anyway, particularly in the evening when the lights are on.

Step 6

Varnish each design carefully with one coat of clear varnish in matt or satin finish. Satin will add a slight sheen whereas matt will protect the design without any shine.

5

6

Bumps and bubbles

The designs may adhere to the wall with slight bumps in them. They will dry flat as the glue or paste dries. If you use wallpaper paste, which is water soluble, you may notice the bumps reappearing as you paint them with the acrylics and varnish. However, these should dry flat within a day of completion.

If any bubbles remain after this, it may mean you have missed a bit with the glue. You can inject a small amount of paste into each bubble with a surgical syringe to fill them.

Stencilled balustrade

This fresh room is stencilled with a stone balustrade. It is painted with exterior paints that contain some sand and gently shaded to give a three-dimensional quality.

Stencilling does not have to be in small-scale country-style hearts and flowers or folk patterns. Try a larger architectural stencil that gives subtle impact to a room. At first glance you do not notice the textured paint used for this balustrade and you will enjoy the element of surprise it has. Put up a stencil below shoulder height in a room and watch how many of your guests touch it. (Peculiar but true!)

As you can imagine, exterior paint is very hard wearing, so your finished work needs no special care; it is washable and simple to repair if it ever does become damaged.

This design is another enlarged photocopy adapted to become a stencil by leaving gaps between the sections of the pillar. Stencil card or plastic is available from craft shops – plastic is a little easier to work with as you can see through it, which helps with lining up. For the top and bottom of the design, which are straight runs along the wall, you will save time by using masking tape instead of cutting this section from the stencil.

The balustrade is a simple design that works to great effect in a room with little furniture. Take a look at the main photograph and imagine how plain this room was before it was stencilled. You can, of course, adjust the colour of your balustrade by mixing artist's acrylic paints into the textured paint.

Planning your time

DAY ONE

AM: Cut stencil; mark positions of pillars around room

PM: Begin stencilling pillars

DAY TWO

AM: Finish stencilling pillars; paint in top and bottom sections

PM: Shade the stencil with crayons

Tools and materials

Design for your stencil (see template on page 73)

Stencil card or plastic

Craft knife

Cutting board or mat

Masking tape (Look out for low-tack tape, which is only half as sticky and does not pull the paint away from the wall as you remove it.)

Cellulose sponges

Small paint roller (optional, but makes life easier)

Fine-textured exterior paint (containing sand) in two colours: light and slightly darker. I used small tester cans; the whole room took 8 of these tester cans – 5 in dark cream and 3 in mid-stone.

Artist's crayons, oil or wax oil (which are harder) in white and yellow ochre or raw sienna

Ruler

Pencil

Spirit level

Something to use as a plumb line (any small weight on the end of a length of string will do – your keys, for example)

1

2

3

Day One

Step 1

Enlarge your design to the required size on a photocopier, bearing in mind that if you already have a dado rail your design must fit snugly between this and the skirting board.

Step 2

Position the design underneath a piece of stencil plastic that is at least twice as big as the design and secure it in place with masking tape.

Step 3

Carefully cut out the design using a craft knife and a metal ruler for the straight edges. Cut two if you are working as a pair. Remember to leave a gap of about 0.5cm (¼ in) between the sections of the balustrade in order that you have separate sections, as can be seen in step 11.

Using a hot pen

If you cut stencils frequently, you might want to invest in a hot pen (available from craft shops). These tools cut through plastic stencil medium like a hot knife through butter. They also get very hot, so are not suitable for children. Cut stencils with a hot pen on a piece of glass, with the design underneath the glass.

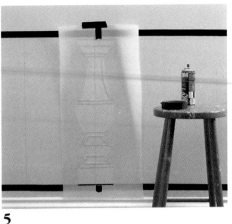

5

4

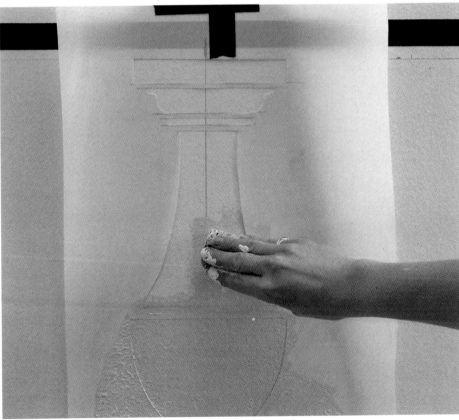

6

Step 4

Now mark the position of your stencils on the wall; do this by marking the top and bottom of each pillar with a straight line or piece of masking tape. Measure an equal distance between each pillar, so that they will be regularly spaced. Lightly mark a vertical line, which will run through the centre of each pillar, using a plumb line and ruler to guide you.

Step 5

Spray the back of the stencil with repositionable spray mount glue and position it carefully on the wall, following the guidelines that mark the centre. Secure the stencil further with small pieces of masking tape.

Step 6

Using a chunk of cellulose sponge or a small paint roller, fill in the whole stencil with the lighter of your chosen colours of textured paint. Leave the stencil in place.

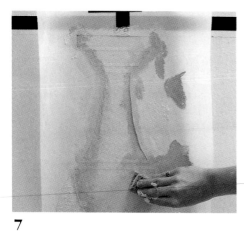

7

Step 7

Now dip a small piece of cellulose sponge into your darker colour and dab off any excess paint onto paper or the edge of the stencil. Dab the darker colour through the stencil to shade it. Shade around the edges and at the bottom of each section of the pillar. Dab the two shades of wet paint together so that your darker shade gently blends into the lighter shade. Then peel away the stencil. Continue stencilling the pillars all around the room. If you are impatient, you can move onto the next step when you have done three or four in order to see your work growing faster.

Day Two

Step 8

Mask off a straight section, along the top of your pillars, leaving no gap, as shown here. Using a cellulose sponge, fill it first with cream paint, and then apply the shading colour along the edges.

Step 9

Repeat step 7 for the bottom section, and the skirting board if your stencil continues down to the floor.

8

9

10

Step 10

When the paint is dry, carefully shade the pillars with crayons to create a three-dimensional effect. Run a thin line of yellow ochre or raw sienna around the edges where the shadows will fall. I crayonned all down the right-hand side of each section, and along the bottom of each. Using a white crayon, add highlights where the light will catch your balustrade and finish creating the three-dimensional effect.

Step 11

You will see that I have run a line of white down the left-hand side of each section, following the curve of the outline, a few centimetres in from the edge. I have also run a line of white along the top of each section.

11

Free-flowing marble bathroom

Sit back in your bathtub and enjoy the flowing and relaxing movements of this simple paint effect that seems to swish and cascade down the walls.

Planning your time

DAY ONE
Mask around the room; paint half of the room

DAY TWO
Paint the second half of the room

Tools and materials

3 x 1 litre cans of eggshell finish paint in your chosen colours

3 x flat trays for the paint (I use large flowerpot holders)

Bristle 'dusting brush' (available from decorating stores and paint merchants) or a wide, bristle decorating brush

White spirit for cleaning up paint

Masking tape

Low cost, low preparation and speedy, this is one of the most popular finishes from my repertoire. It is a super treatment for walls that are already painted or have paper on them that is still in good condition. This is not a lesson in how to imitate marble – good marbling takes more than a weekend to master. It is a decoration inspired by the look of natural marbles, but uses no glazes or specialist brushes. It is not even a very messy job.

Once you get started, this free-flowing marble effect does not even require much concentration. So where is the catch? You need to expend a great deal of energy – all the stippling required can make your arm ache – but it is a small price to pay for such a beautiful finish.

Your walls need to be quite smooth (a few bumps do not matter), and painted or papered in a paler shade than the colours you choose to use. I recommend you give patterned papers a coat or two of white emulsion before starting, just in case the pattern shows through the new paint.

When selecting your colours, keep to three shades of the same colour. When you blend these together on the wall you will create a myriad of shades. If you select different colours you may find that they blend to become muddy shades. Yellow and blue lines, for example, will blend into green; red and green will blend to brown.

Step 1

Prepare your room for painting by making sure that the walls are clean. Mask off any fixtures such as taps, light switches and the point at which the walls meet the ceiling. Prepare three flat trays of paint with only about 1 cm (½ in) depth of paint in each tray. I have used eggshell paint for two reasons: first, eggshell paint is water resistant when dry and is therefore excellent for bathrooms; and second, it dries more slowly than emulsion and offers more time for blending. You can use another type of paint if you prefer.

Step 2

To apply the paint dip the very tip of the dusting brush into the tray of colour. Start with the darkest of your colours. It is important that you do not overload your brush; if any paint drips from the brush, dab it off on a piece of paper before you start stippling.

Step 3

Working in patches about 60 cm (2 ft) across, or larger once you get going, hold your brush as shown here, with the long side following the direction of your intended 'flow'. Stipple the paint onto the wall with a sharp but light jabbing motion. Follow a general, wiggly diagonal flow. If you are using similar colours to here, go easy on the darkest shade. The only shapes to avoid when making these squiggles are any large cross shapes or noticeable 'X' shapes. If you do make any of these by mistake you can quickly blend them out with the other shades of paint.

1   2

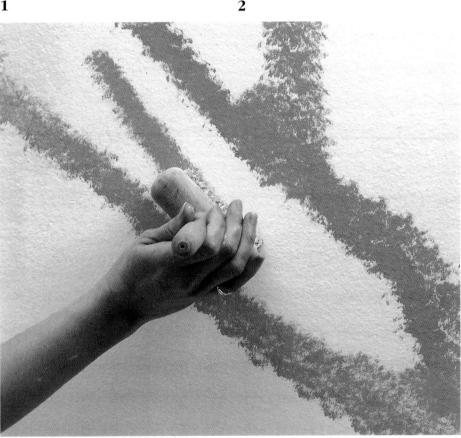

3

Looking after your brush

If you take a break from your work for more than a few minutes, there is no need to wash your brush. Simply wrap it in foil or plastic to stop it from drying out. Wash your brush before leaving it overnight.

4

5

Step 4

When you have run out of paint on your brush, immediately dip the tip into the mid shade and apply some diagonally flowing lines to the wall next to your dark lines. Blend the two colours together where they meet by dabbing the brush into the dark lines, which will still be wet, and back into the lighter shade. Once again, avoid obvious crossovers.

Step 5

Now repeat the process with the lightest shade of paint (here I have used white), filling in all the spaces and blending into both colours.

Step 6

Finally, stand back from the wall and check that your colours are well blended. Add extra lines in any shade where you think necessary. Look for obvious marks left by the jabbing motion of your brush and gently stipple them away. Repeat steps 4 and 5 and blending until all the walls are covered. Wash out the brush and remove the masking tape.

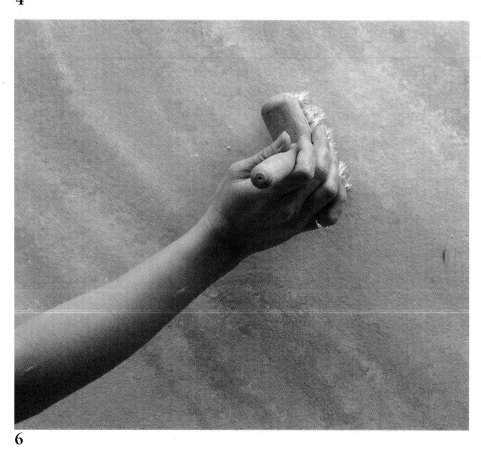

6

Adjusting the finish

After the paint is dry, if you see an area with which you are not happy you can adjust it simply by stippling over some fresh paint.

Painted and stencilled tiles

Here is a great way of sprucing up your tiled walls without having to go to the expense and complication of replacing them – just paint and stencil them.

At last there are products on the market which mean you can paint those old tiles in your kitchen or bathroom. This cheery yellow kitchen was dark green before the painting started. The tiles have been given a basic and very speedy colourwash and then stencilled with a vegetable motif to echo the fun design on the curtains.

The main ingredient that allows you to paint tiles successfully is a 'tile primer' paint. It is incredibly hard wearing and difficult to chip or damage once it is fully dry. Tile primer provides a base for normal emulsion or eggshell paints. The primer takes a long while to dry, however, so this project will demand your attention on the evening before your weekend decoration. You will be finished, though, by the end of the morning of the third day.

If your tiled room is small and you would like it to look bigger, then avoid shades of red or orange. These are 'advancing' colours and can make a room look a little smaller (and cosier). Fresh green is a receding colour, as are fresh blues so these colours can add a feeling of space. Blue can look quite cold in a kitchen or bathroom, though, particularly if the windows do not face direct sunlight. All that said, this kitchen is painted yellow for no other reason than the fact that I like yellow!

Planning your time

DAY ONE
Evening: Paint the tiles with primer

DAY TWO
AM: Paint primed tiles; paint wall above tiles

PM: Colourwash tiles; paint dado

DAY THREE
AM: Apply stencils

Tools and materials

2 litres of tile primer (available from DIY stores)

Good quality synthetic brush

Small synthetic roller (the type sold for gloss paint is good)

2.5 litres of white vinyl silk emulsion

2.5 litres of emulsion paint in your chosen colour for the area above the tiles

1 litre of transparent scumble glaze (oil or water based; I used oil based)

1 litre of eggshell paint in your chosen colourwash colour (if you are using water-based glaze see page 71)

White spirit

Good quality decorator's brush

Stencils
(see templates on pages 74–75)

Selection of acrylic artist's paints for stencilling

Small sponge for stencilling (the type of sponges sold for babies are perfect for stencilling as they are smooth)

Day One

Step 1

Ensure that your tiles are clean. Paint them with one good coat of tile primer. The manufacturers recommend the use of a synthetic brush for this. I have to confess, however, that I used a small roller for the main areas, which I found to be quicker and to leave a pleasing 'stippled' effect on the walls. Do not worry if the colour of the old tiles shows through the paint slightly, but do take care to cover the entire tiled area without leaving any gaps. Leave the primer to dry overnight.

Day Two

Step 2

Paint the tiles with two coats of white vinyl silk emulsion paint (not matt). If the first coat of paint is not dry enough to re-paint by the time you have worked your way all around the room, move on to step 3 and come back to apply the second coat when it is dry.

Step 3

Paint the wall above the tiles with two coats of emulsion paint. Vinyl silk is more washable than matt finish paint and may be best to use for a kitchen or bathroom.

1

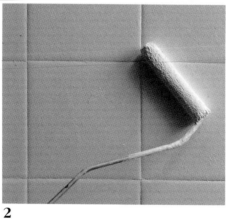

2

3

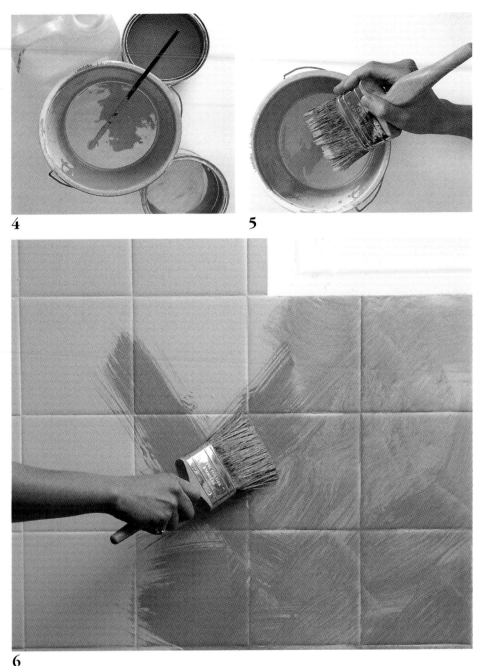

4

5

6

Step 4

Mix your colourwash glaze with 0.25 litres of transparent oil-based glaze, 0.25 litres of eggshell paint in your selected colour and 0.25 litres of white spirit. The mix should be as thin as milk and no thicker than single cream. If it is too thick add more white spirit. Stir the glaze well.

Step 5

Start the colourwashing by first dipping the very tip of the dry brush into the glaze. Paint should not drip from the brush. If it does, wipe the excess away on a piece of paper.

Step 6

Apply the glaze to the wall in broad criss-cross strokes. The main feature of this basic colourwashing is the fact that the brush strokes show. This is a very random effect and it does not matter in which direction your brush strokes go, as long as you are happy with them; there are no rights or wrongs. Leave small areas of the white base paint showing through the glaze. If you want to see how your colourwashing will look you can test it on a piece of paper or painted board.

Working with glaze

Do not leave a wall half colourwashed or you will see a 'watermark' where the glaze overlaps after you come back to it. Stop only at corners. Glaze starts to dry in only a few minutes, so you have to work fast.

Applying a second layer of colourwash

If you would like your colourwashing to have more depth to it, allow the first coat to dry and then repeat steps 5 and 6 with a second layer. Two-coat colourwashing looks tidier than one coat.

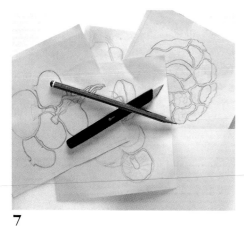

7

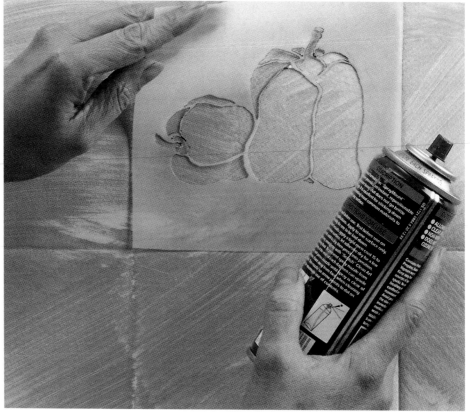

Day Three

Step 7

If you are not using the templates on pages 74–75, and want to design your own stencil, keep it simple. Break a large area into smaller sections before cutting it out as a stencil. Different parts, such as for leaves and fruits, must be separated by a gap or 'bridge' in the stencil. (See page 58 of the Stencilled balustrade project for guidelines on cutting out stencils.)

8

Step 8

Once your colourwashing is dry, position your stencil on the wall using repositionable spray mount (sprayed lightly onto the back of the stencil). A heavy stencil will also need a piece of masking tape to hold it in place.

Step 9

Prepare a palette (or old plate) of artist's acrylic colours and dip a small section of sponge into the paint. Dab a couple of times onto the palette to remove excess paint and then dab the paint through the stencil to colour it.

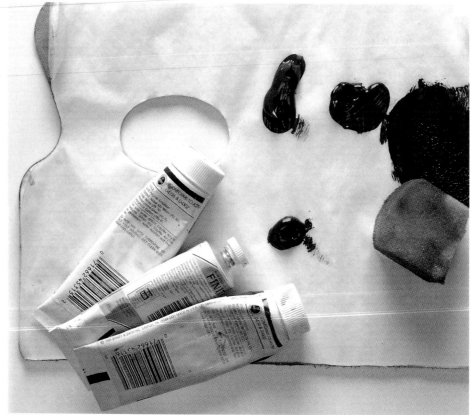

9

10

Step 10

You will find that you can blend the paints quite easily with the sponge while they are still wet. I used alizarin crimson with a touch of raw umber mixed into it for the red peppers, sap green and raw umber for the greens and added a good squirt of white for the leek design. For the onions I used raw umber, burnt sienna and white. Peel away the stencil and paint the roots on by hand if you wish.

Step 11

Finally, if you have a dado rail, give it a fresh coat of paint in the same eggshell as you used to mix the glaze.

11

Using water-based glaze

If you prefer to work with water-based glaze, ask your supplier for the glaze that you can colour with emulsion paint. Mix in the same way as for oil-based glaze (1 part glaze, 1 part paint) and use water to thin it.

Templates

Frottage on a Roman vase

Templates

Photocopied designs for a study

Stencilled balustrade

Templates

Painted and stencilled tiles

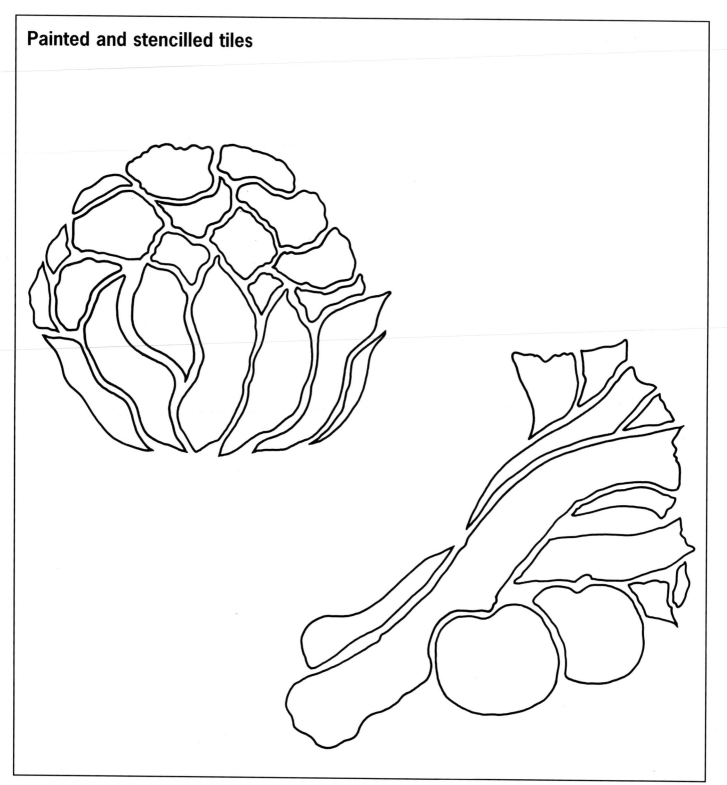

Templates

Painted and stencilled tiles

Glossary

Artist's oil colours

Available in tubes from art shops, these paints consist of crushed pigments mixed with linseed oil to make them creamy in texture. Artist's oil colours dry very slowly.

Artist's palette

A flat board onto which you can mix artist's paints. It is shaped so that you can hold it comfortably in one hand. Available in plastic, wood or paper pads that are disposable.

Beading
Ready-made ornate strips of wood for use as panels, dados etc.

Border adhesive
Glue made specifically for attaching paper borders to a wall.

Cellulose sponges
Brightly coloured synthetic sponges sold in supermarkets and DIY stores.

Colourizers

Small bottles of colour for staining acrylic scumble glaze.

Commercial borders

Narrow rolls of pre-printed paper, designed for decorative use around a room at ceiling, picture rail or dado height. Available from all wallpaper suppliers.

Concrete
A mixture of sand and cement powder.

Decorating brush
It is worth buying a good quality brush, preferably made of bristle. Avoid brushes that have a space in the centre of the bristles where a wedge of wood has been pushed in. This wedge is a manufacturer's trick to make the brush look thicker than it really is. The paint gathers in the space and will drip from your brush.

Decorative moulding glue
A faster bonding glue than PVA.

Découpage
Decoration of surfaces with paper cut-outs.

Dragging brush

A long-haired brush specially designed for making the delicate striped effect of dragging.

Dryers
A chemical additive that speeds up the drying time of paint.

Dusting brush

A thick, wide brush, made of bristle. Used by decorators for flicking away dust from an article to be painted. Used here for stippling on paint as they are less expensive than genuine stippling brushes and have the same effect.

Eggshell paint
Oil-based, satin-finish paint.

Gilder's size
The glue used in gilding. You will find a variety of drying times for gilder's size from 20 minutes to 24 hours – choose one that is quick drying.

Gold paints

Available in tubes from art shops. Acrylic dries much faster than oils, which can take some days to dry.

Hook and loop fastener
Supplied in rolls, this has two sections, one comprising of many firm, flexible hooks that grip

into the other section, comprising hundreds of tiny loops. A popular method for joining two pieces of fabric and available from needlework stores.

Medium density fibreboard (MDF)
Strong board made from soft wood fibres bonded together under pressure. It is sanded to produce an extremely smooth surface.

Mitre block
A block designed to help cut diagonal angles for corners etc. (from wood or plaster). It has a ready-cut slot to guide your saw.

Panel glue
Glue made for fixing coving and panels etc. to walls. It is supplied in a large tube with a gun for applying it with.

Paint roller
These are ideal when you are painting large surface areas. Look out for patterned foam rollers that create an interesting texture on a flat surface.

PVA/EVA glue
White woodworking and general purpose adhesive that dries clear. EVA is the waterproof type.

Rottenstone
A fine grey powder pigment used for dirtying and ageing.

Scumble glaze
A medium that when mixed with ordinary paints makes them slippery in texture. This allows you to manipulate the colour on the wall into interesting patterns. Usually available as water based or oil based, it can be bought from any paint suppliers who supplies materials for marbling and paint effects. Acrylic scumble is also available, but you need to work fast as acrylic glaze dries quickly.

Staple gun
A gun that shoots staples into walls or wood with great force.

Stipple
A paint technique using the tips of the brush in a jabbing movement, producing a textured surface to the paint.

Tenon saw
A short, fine-toothed saw. If you are buying a new saw choose one that is as long as possible as this will give you a longer sweep with each cut and the work will be faster.

Tesserae
Mosaic tiles.

Tile primer
Water-based paint for painting tiles. It has excellent adhesion. and is quite thick and sticky in texture.

Transfer leaf
Fine sheets of gilder's metal on a piece of backing paper.

Transparent oil glaze
The correct name for oil-based scumble glaze.

Varnishing brush
A flat brush specifically designed for varnishing but useful for all paintwork. Varnishing brushes hold a large amount of paint and have very fine bristles.

Wooden frames for fabric panels
The basic wooden structure onto which fabric is stretched for making fabric panels. The frames should be strengthened with at least two cross-bars each to help them to keep their shape.

Suppliers

Thanks to the following for supplying equipment, paints, papers and furniture:

Akzo Nobel Decorative Coatings
Hollins Road, Darwen,
Lancashire BB3 OBG
Anaglypta® wall covering.

And So to Bed
638-640 King's Road, London SW6 2DU
(Tel. 0171 731 3593)
Bedlinen, divan and mattress in cheat's découpage project page 23.

ARC
103 Wandsworth Bridge Road,
London SW6 2TE
(Tel. 0171 731 3933)
Framed prints page 19.

Atlantis Art
146 Brick Lane, London E1 6RU
(Tel. 0171 377 8855)
Europe's biggest art supplies store.

C. Brewer and Sons Ltd
Head office: Albany House,
Ashford Road, Eastbourne,
East Sussex BN21 3TR
(Tel. 01323 411080)
Paint supplies for projects throughout the book.

Jane Churchill
151 Sloane Street, London SW1X 9BX
(Tel. 0171 730 9847)
Curtain fabric 'Dancing Vegetables' in painted tiles project page 67.

The Classic Chair Company Ltd
The Old Imperial Laundry, 71 Warriner Gardens, London SW11 4XU
(Tel. 0171 622 4274)
Console table and accessories in accent colours project page 33.

Crucial Trading at Pukka Palace
174 Tower Bridge Road, London SE1
(Tel. 0171 234 0000)
Coir and sisal flooring throughout, plus furniture in stone wall project page 27.

Depitch Designs
7 College Fields, Prince George's Road,
London SW19 2PT
(Tel. 0181 687 0867)
Headboard in cheat's découpage project page 23.

The Design Archives
The Decorative Fabrics Gallery,
278-280 Brompton Road,
London SW3 2AS
(Tel. 0171 589 4778)
Fabric panels.

The Furniture Cave
1st Floor, 533 King's Road,
London SW10 OTZ
(Tel. 0171 352 4229)

Habitat
(Tel. 0645 334433 for branches)
Accessories throughout.

Jali Ltd
Apsley House, Chartham, Canterbury,
Kent CT4 7HT
(Tel. 01227 831710)
MDF trimmings and radiator box, contemporary dado project page 19.

Brian McClure
Tower Bridge Studios, 59-60 Stanworth Street, London SE1
(Tel. 0171 231 4044)
Wooden printing block collage page 33.

E. Ploton
273 Archway Road, London N6 5AA
(Tel. 0181 348 2838)
Art supplies, glazes, rottenstone, wax oil crayons and gilding supplies.

Polyvine Ltd
Vine House, Rockhampton, Berkely,
Gloucestershire GL13 9DT
(Tel. 01454 261276)
Acrylic scumble glaze and colourizers.

Purves and Purves
81–83 Tottenham Court Road,
London W1P 9HD
(Tel. 0171 580 8223)
*Desk, chair and accessories in
photocopied designs project page 53.*

J. H. Ratcliffe and Sons
135a Linaker Street,
Southport PR8 5DF
(Tel. 01704 537999)
Transparent oil glaze.

Suzanne Ruggles
(Tel. 0181 542 8476 for more details)
*Torchère vase in stencilling project
page 57.*

Sanderson
112 Brompton Rd, London SW3 1JJ
(Tel. 0171 584 3344)
Cushions in frottage project page 9.

Spode China
(Tel. 01782 744011 for stockists)
China throughout.

Steamer Furniture
The Forge, Wigmore, Leominster,
Herefordshire HR6 9UA
(Tel. 01568 770462)
*Steamer chair and table, frottage
project page 9.*

Succession
179 Westbourne Grove, London W11
(Tel. 0171 727 0580)
*Leather chair in accent colours project
page 33.*

Edgar Udney
314 Balham High Road,
London SW17 7AA
(Tel. 0181 767 8181)
Mosaic supplies.

The Water Monopoly
16–18 Lonsdale Road, London NW6
(Tel. 0171 624 2636)
Baths and taps.

Index